G. SCHIRMER'S
COLLECTION OF
OPERA LIBRETTOS

SALOME

Music Drama in One Act
(After Oscar Wilde's Tragedy)

Music by

Richard Strauss

English Version by
CHARLES POLACHEK

Ed. 2585

G. SCHIRMER, Inc.

DISTRIBUTED BY

HAL•LEONARD®

SALOME

When Richard Strauss was born in Munich in 1864, Wagner's patron, King Ludwig II of Bavaria, was still reigning monarch. Strauss' father, a horn player in the court orchestra, thought little of Wagner and in his son's early musical training he stressed the classics of Haydn, Mozart, Beethoven and Brahms. The boy, precocious if not a prodigy, studied piano with his mother from the age of four and learned musical notation before written words. As a young man, Strauss showed a decided predilection for romantic influences, such as Mendelssohn and Schumann, in his composition. He was nearing nineteen when Wagner died and little dreamed that he would one day be the master's heir in German music drama.

By the time he produced his first opera, *Guntram* (1894), he was resolutely under Wagner's influence. The work, based on the style of *Parsifal,* failed completely, but his next opera, *Feuersnot,* seven years later and less derivatively Wagnerian, proved a fair success. In *Feuersnot* Strauss hit upon two of his most effective devices: satire and shock. The latter may have guided his strong attraction to Oscar Wilde's play *Salome,* which he saw that same year, 1901. His almost word for word musical setting of the Wilde text marks Strauss' emergence as a mature, individualistic composer. Highly symphonic in concept and treatment, it permits a tone-poem-like structure to follow the play's form. Though the composer's colleagues affected horror at the libretto's "decadent" subject matter, they were more disturbed by the sensuous, erotic music, which disregarded every traditional concept of theater and beauty.

Since the Biblical story of Herod's stepdaughter is brief, writers have been free to interpret it in various ways. (Another operatic setting, Jules Massenet's *Hérodiade,* has John the Baptist fall in love with Salome!) Wilde's text gives the story no moral, the standard procedure up to his time. The playwright's perception of Salome's psychopathological nature permits the heroine's character to develop, within a short time, from seeming naïveté to overt degeneration. Strauss underlined this swift change in a jarring musical tour de force that fused word and music.

Censors forbade that the world premiere of *Salome* take place in Vienna, the Kaiser cancelled a projected Berlin production and London did not hear the work as originally planned. The first performance was given at the Dresden Royal Opera on December 9, 1905, with Marie Wittich in the title role; declining to conduct himself, Strauss assigned the podium to Ernst von Schuch. The American premiere, at the Metropolitan Opera House on January 22, 1907, scandalized New York. Olive Fremstad, who sang Salome, had visited the local morgue to find out the actual weight of a human head. At the first performance, as she lifted the platter containing the paper machee head of Jokanaan on high, she staggered so realistically that several horrified subscribers fled the theater. The next day the critics called Marion Weede's Herodias a "human hyena" and Carl Burrian's Herod a "neurasthenic voluptuary." *Salome,* denounced from the pulpit and in print, was withdrawn immediately and did not return to the boards of the Metropolitan for twenty-seven years. Today, Strauss' one-act shocker retains its impact and is in the repertory whenever a soprano is available who can sing and dance the gruelling title role.

THE STORY

On a moonlit terrace of King Herod's palace in Judea, Narraboth, a young captain of the guard, gazes rapturously at the beautiful princess Salome, who feasts with her stepfather Herod and his court in the banquet hall. Though a page warns him not to stare so intently at the princess lest something terrible happen, he fails to rouse Narraboth from his trance. The voice of Jokanaan proclaiming the Messiah's greatness is heard from a deep cistern, where he has been imprisoned by the king; two soldiers comment on the prophet's kindness and Herod's fear of him. Suddenly Narraboth exclaims that Salome is approaching. The princess, bored by Herod's lecherous glances and the brutality of the Romans, seeks a breath of air in the cool moonlight. Soon the voice of Jokanaan sounds again, this time hurling curses at the sinful Herodias. Salome's curiosity is aroused, but the soldiers refuse her request that they open the cistern and allow her to speak with the prophet; at this she turns her wiles on Narraboth who, unable to resist her, orders that Jokanaan be allowed forth. First terrified by the sight of the austere prophet, who denounces her mother anew, Salome grows fascinated by the deathly pallor of his body. Despite the protests of Narraboth, the princess pours forth her uncontrollable desire to touch the hair, skin and lips of the holy man. Jokanaan rejects each of her passionate outbursts. While Narraboth, in horror and despair, stabs himself, Salome sinks in frustration at the feet of the prophet, who urges her to save herself by seeking Christ. When she continues to beg for his kiss, Jokanaan retreats into the cistern, proclaiming her accursed. Beside herself with unfulfilled longing, the girl falls exhausted upon the cistern.

Looking for Salome, Herod comes forth, shortly followed by his court; commenting on the strange look of the moon, he slips in Narraboth's blood and, unnerved, falls victim to hallucinations. Herodias scornfully dismisses his fantasies and suggests that he withdraw with her, but Herod's attentions have meanwhile focused on Salome. Though he tries to win her favor with offers of food and wine, the princess spurns his advances. Renewed abuses from Jokanaan harrass Herodias, who demands that Herod turn the prophet over to the Jews; Herod refuses, maintaining that Jokanaan is a holy man and has seen God. At these words an argument breaks out between five Jews concerning the true nature of God, after which two Nazarenes report the miracles of Jesus. As Jokanaan continues his denunciation of Herodias, the queen furiously commands his silence. Herod, seeking diversion, asks Salome to dance for him. She refuses, but when he promises as reward anything she desires, the girl consents, first making him swear to live up to his bargain. Fear again seizes the king, who tears a garland of roses from his feverish brow as Herodias begs Salome not to dance. Ignoring her mother's pleas, the princess performs a dance with seven veils, finally falling naked at Herod's feet. When the delighted monarch asks what reward she wishes, with the innocence of a child she asks that the head of Jokanaan be brought her on a silver platter. Horrified, the king refuses, while Herodias laughs approval at Salome's choice. In desperation, Herod suggests alternative rewards: the world's most beautiful emerald, his rare white peacocks, even the sacred veil of the sanctuary. But Salome's demand grows more and more insistent until the king wearily gives in to her request. As an executioner descends into the cistern, Salome peers over the edge, awaiting her prize; just when she believes the slave has betrayed her, his arm rises from the cistern bearing the prophet's head on a silver platter. Salome seizes her reward, passionately addressing Jokanaan as though he still lived. Terrified, Herod whispers to Herodias that her daughter is a monster. Ominous clouds fill the sky as the king rises to enter the palace. When the torches are extinguished, a stray moonbeam falls on the princess; having kissed Jokanaan's lips, she moans in the ecstasy of her triumph. Herod, turning on the staircase, orders the soldiers to kill the princess. They crush her beneath their shields.

Courtesy Opera News

CAST OF CHARACTERS

HEROD ANTIPAS, TETRARCH OF JUDEA . . . . Tenor

HERODIAS, WIFE OF THE TETRARCH . . . . Mezzosoprano

SALOME, DAUGHTER OF HERODIAS . . . . Soprano

JOKANAAN, THE PROPHET . . . . Baritone

NARRABOTH, A YOUNG SYRIAN . . . . Tenor

THE PAGE OF HERODIAS . . . . Contralto

FIVE JEWS . . . . ⎰ 4 Tenors
⎱ 1 Bass

TWO NAZARENES . . . . ⎰ Tenor
⎱ Bass

TWO SOLDIERS ⎱
A CAPPADOCIAN ⎰ . . . . Basses

A SLAVE

PLACE: A grand terrace in the Palace of Herod

SALOME

Eine grosse Terrasse im Palast des Herodes, die an den Bankettsaal stösst.

(*Einige Soldaten lehnen sich über die Brüstung. Rechts eine mächtige Treppe, links im Hintergrund eine alte Cisterne mit einer Einfassung aus grüner Bronze. Der Mond scheint sehr hell.*)

NARRABOTH

Wie schön ist Prinzessin Salome heute nacht!

PAGE

Sieh die Mondscheibe, wie sie seltsam aussieht. Wie eine Frau, die aufsteigt aus dem Grab.

NARRABOTH

Sie ist sehr seltsam. Wie eine kleine Prinzessin, deren Füsse weisse Tauben sind. Man könnte meinen, sie tanzt.

PAGE

Wie eine Frau, die tot ist. Sie gleitet langsam dahin.

(*Lärm im Bankettsaal*)

ERSTER SOLDAT

Was für ein Aufruhr! Was sind das für wilde Tiere, die da heulen?

ZWEITER SOLDAT

Die Juden.
(*trocken*)
Sie sind immer so. Sie streiten über ihre Religion.

ERSTER SOLDAT

Ich finde es lächerlich, über solche Dinge zu streiten.

NARRABOTH

Wie schön ist Prinzessin Salome heute abend!

PAGE

Du siehst sie immer an. Du siehst sie zuviel an. Es ist gefährlich, Menschen auf diese Art anzusehn. Schreckliches kann geschehn.

NARRABOTH

Sie ist sehr schön heute abend.

ERSTER SOLDAT

Der Tetrarch sieht finster drein.

ZWEITER SOLDAT

Ja, er sieht finster drein.

ERSTER SOLDAT

Auf wen blickt er?

ZWEITER SOLDAT

Ich weiss nicht.

NARRABOTH

Wie blass die Prinzessin ist. Niemals habe ich sie so blass gesehn. Sie ist wie der Schatten einer weissen Rose in einem silbernen Spiegel.

PAGE (*sehr unruhig*)

Du musst sie nicht ansehn. Du siehst sie zuviel an. Schreckliches kann geschehn.

DIE STIMME DES IOCHANAAN
(*aus der Cisterne*)

Nach mir wird Einer kommen, der ist stärker als ich. Ich bin nicht wert, ihm zu lösen den Riemen an seinen Schuh'n. Wenn er kommt, werden die verödeten Stätten frohlocken. Wenn er kommt, werden die Augen der Blinden den Tag sehn. Wenn er kommt, die Ohren der Tauben geöffnet.

ZWEITER SOLDAT

Heiss' ihn schweigen!

ERSTER SOLDAT

Er ist ein heil'ger Mann.

ZWEITER SOLDAT

Er sagt immer lächerliche Dinge.

ERSTER SOLDAT

Er ist sehr sanft. Jeden Tag, den ich ihm zu essen gebe, dankt er mir.

EIN CAPPADOCIER

Wer ist es?

ERSTER SOLDAT

Ein Prophet.

SALOME

A grand terrace in the Palace of Herod, set above the banquet hall.

(*Some soldiers are leaning over the balcony. To the right there is a gigantic staircase; to the left, at the back, an old cistern surrounded by a wall of green bronze. The moon is shining very brightly.*)

NARRABOTH

How beautiful the Princess Salome is tonight!

PAGE

See the moon shining. She has such a strange look! She's like a woman rising from a tomb.

NARRABOTH

She has a strange look. She is much like a princess who has feet as white as turtle doves. You would believe she was dancing.

PAGE

She's like a long dead woman. She moves so slowly along.

(*noise in the banquet hall*)

FIRST SOLDIER

What an uproar! Who is howling like the jackals of the desert?

SECOND SOLDIER (*dryly*)

The Hebrews.
They are all like that. They quarrel about their religion.

FIRST SOLDIER

I find it ridiculous to argue over such matters.

NARRABOTH

How beautiful the Princess Salome is this evening!

PAGE

You always look at her. You look too much at her. It's very dangerous to look at a human face in such a way. Terrible things may come.

NARRABOTH

She is so fair on this evening.

FIRST SOLDIER

See how grim the Tetrarch looks.

SECOND SOLDIER

Yes, he's a somber look.

FIRST SOLDIER

At whom does he look?

SECOND SOLDIER

I don't know.

NARRABOTH

How pale is the Princess. I have never seen her as pale as this! She is like a shadow of a snow white rose in a mirror of silver.

PAGE (*very restless*)

You must not look at her. You look too much at her. Terrible things may come.

VOICE OF JOKANAAN
(*from the cistern*)

Then there will come another who is greater than I. I am not worthy to loosen the latchet of his shoes. When he comes, then shall the deserted places be green again. When he comes, shall the eyes of the blind see the daylight. When he comes, the ears of the deaf shall be open.

SECOND SOLDIER

Bid him be silent!

FIRST SOLDIER

He is a Holy man.

SECOND SOLDIER

He keeps saying things which sound ridiculous.

FIRST SOLDIER

But he is good. Every day when I bring him food he thanks me with kindly words.

CAPPADOCIAN

Who is he?

FIRST SOLDIER

He's a prophet.

1

EIN CAPPADOCIER

Wie ist sein Name?

ERSTER SOLDAT

Iochanaan.

EIN CAPPADOCIER

Woher kommt er?

ERSTER SOLDAT

Aus der Wüste. Eine Schar von Jüngern war dort immer um ihn.

EIN CAPPADOCIER

Wovon redet er?

ERSTER SOLDAT

Unmöglich ist's, zu verstehn, was er sagt.

EIN CAPPADOCIER

Kann man ihn sehn?

ERSTER SOLDAT

Nein, der Tetrarch hat es verboten.

NARRABOTH (*sehr erregt*)

Die Prinzessin erhebt sich! Sie verlässt die Tafel. Sie ist sehr erregt. Sie kommt hierher.

PAGE

Sieh sie nicht an!

NARRABOTH

Ja, sie kommt auf uns zu.

PAGE

Ich bitte dich, sieh sie nicht an!

NARRABOTH

Sie ist wie eine verirrte Taube.

(*Salome tritt erregt ein*)

SALOME

Ich will nicht bleiben. Ich kann nicht bleiben. Warum sieht mich der Tetrarch fortwährend so an mit seinen Maulwurfsaugen unter den zuckenden Lidern? Es ist seltsam, dass der Mann meiner Mutter mich so ansieht. Wie süss ist hier die Luft! Hier kann ich atmen. Da drinnen sitzen Juden aus Jerusalem, die einander über ihre närrischen Gebräuche in Stücke reissen. Schweigsame, list'ge Aegypter und brutale ungeschlachte Römer mit ihrer plumpen Sprache. O, wie ich diese Römer hasse.

PAGE (*zu Narraboth*)

Schreckliches wird geschehn Warum siehst du sie so an?

SALOME

Wie gut ist's, in den Mond zu sehn. Er ist wie eine silberne Blume, kühl und keusch. Ja, wie die Schönheit einer Jungfrau, die rein geblieben ist.

DIE STIMME DES JOCHANAAN

Siehe, der Herr ist gekommen, des Menchen Sohn ist nahe.

SALOME

Wer war das, der hier gerufen hat?

ZWEITER SOLDAT

Der Prophet, Prinzessin.

SALOME

Ach, der Prophet! Der, vor dem der Tetrarch Angst hat?

ZWEITER SOLDAT

Wir wissen davon nichts, Prinzessin. Es war der Prophet Iochanaan, der hier rief.

NARRABOTH (*zu Salome*)

Beliebt es Euch, dass ich Eure Sänfte holen lasse, Prinzessin? Die Nacht ist schön im Garten.

SALOME

Er sagt schreckliche Dinge über meine Mutter, nicht wahr?

ZWEITER SOLDAT

Wir verstehen nie, was er sagt, Prinzessin.

SALOME

Ja, er sagt schreckliche Dinge über sie.

(*Ein Sklave tritt ein.*)

SKLAVE

Prinzessin, der Tetrarch ersucht Euch, wieder zum Fest hineinzugehn.

SALOME (*heftig*)

Ich will nicht hineingehn.

(*Der Sklave geht ab.*)

Ist dieser Prophet ein alter Mann?

NARRABOTH (*dringender*)

Prinzessin, es wäre besser hineinzugehn. Gestattet, dass ich Euch führe.

SALOME (*gesteigert*)

Ist der Prophet ein alter Mann?

CAPPADOCIAN

What do they call him?

FIRST SOLDIER

Jokanaan.

CAPPADOCIAN

And whence comes he?

FIRST SOLDIER

From the desert. And a crowd assembled and stayed to hear his words.

CAPPADOCIAN

Of what does he talk?

FIRST SOLDIER

Not one of us understands what he says.

CAPPADOCIAN

May he be seen?

FIRST SOLDIER

No, 'tis forbidden by the Tetrarch.

NARRABOTH (*very excited*)

Now the Princess is rising! She is leaving the table! She looks very strange. She's coming out.

PAGE

Don't look at her!

NARRABOTH

Yes, she's coming out here.

PAGE

I beg of you, don't look at her!

NARRABOTH

She is like a bewildered, lost dove.

SALOME (*enters excited*)

I will not stay there! I cannot stay there. And why does the Tetrarch watch me all the while out of those mole's eyes from under his quivering eyelids. It is most strange that the husband of my mother looks at me like that! How sweet is the air here. Here I can breathe. Within are sitting Hebrews from Jerusalem who will quarrel with each other until all their garments are torn to pieces. Silent and subtle Egyptians, and those brutal and barbaric Romans who speak an uncouth jargon. Oh, how much I hate these Romans!

PAGE (*to Narraboth*)

Terrible things will come. Do not look so much at her.

SALOME

How lovely is the moon tonight. She's like a little flower of silver, cool and chaste. She has the beauty of a virgin, so pure and undefiled.

VOICE OF JOKANAAN

Lift up thine eyes to the mountains, the Son of God is coming.

SALOME

Who was that? Who was that crying out?

SECOND SOLDIER

'Twas the prophet, Princess.

SALOME

Ah, 'twas the prophet, he whom the Tetrarch is afraid of!

SECOND SOLDIER

We know nothing of that, my Princess. It was the prophet Jokanaan whom you heard.

NARRABOTH (*to Salome*)

Is it your pleasure that I bid them bring your litter, my Princess? The night is fair in the garden.

SALOME

He tells terrible stories all about my mother, does he not?

SECOND SOLDIER

We cannot understand what he says, my Princess.

SALOME

Yes, he tells terrible stories about her.

SLAVE (*entering*)

My Princess, the Tetrarch calls you. Will you return to the feast again?

SALOME (*passionately*)

I will not go back now.

(*The slave leaves.*)

This prophet, is he an old man?

NARRABOTH (*urgently*)

My Princess, it will be better to return again. Allow me to lead you back now.

SALOME (*eagerly*)

This prophet, is he an old man?

ERSTER SOLDAT

Nein, Prinzessin, er ist ganz jung.

DIE STIMME DES JOCHANAAN

Jauchze nicht, du Land Palästina, weil der Stab dessen, der dich schlug, gebrochen ist. Denn aus dem Samen der Schlange wird ein Basilisk kommen, und seine Brut wird die Vögel verschlingen.

SALOME

Welch seltsame Stimme! Ich möchte mit ihm sprechen.

ZWEITER SOLDAT

Prinzessin, der Tetrarch duldet nicht, dass irgend wer mit ihm spricht. Er hat selbst dem Hohenpriester verboten, mit ihm zu sprechen.

SALOME

Ich wünsche mit ihm zu sprechen.

ZWEITER SOLDAT

Es ist unmöglich, Prinzessin.

SALOME (*immer heftiger*)

Ich will mit ihm sprechen. Bringt diesen Propheten heraus!

ZWEITER SOLDAT

Wir dürfen nicht, Prinzessin.

SALOME

(*tritt an die Cisterne heran und blickt hinunter*)

Wie schwarz es da drunten ist! Es muss schrecklich sein, in so einer schwarzen Höhle zu leben. Es ist wie eine Gruft.

(*wild*)

Habt ihr nicht gehört? Bringt den Propheten heraus! Ich möchte ihn sehn!

ERSTER SOLDAT

Prinzessin, wir dürfen nicht tun, was Ihr von uns begehrt.

SALOME (*erblickt Narraboth*)

Ah!

PAGE

O, was wird geschehn? Ich weiss, es wird Schreckliches geschehn.

SALOME

(*tritt an Narraboth heran, leise und lebhaft sprechend*)

Du wirst das für mich tun, Narraboth, nicht wahr? Ich war dir immer gewogen. Du wirst das für mich tun. Ich möchte ihn bloss sehn, diesen seltsamen Propheten. Die Leute haben soviel von ihm gesprochen. Ich glaube, der Tetrarch hat Angst vor ihm.

NARRABOTH

Der Tetrarch hat es ausdrücklich verboten, dass irgend wer den Deckel zu diesem Brunnen aufhebt.

SALOME

Du wirst das für mich tun, Narraboth, (*sehr hastig*) und morgen, wenn ich in meiner Sänfte an dem Torweg, wo die Götzenbilder stehn, vorbeikomme, werde ich eine kleine Blume für dich fallen lassen, ein kleines grünes Blümchen.

NARRABOTH

Prinzessin, ich kann nicht, ich kann nicht.

SALOME (*bestimmter*)

Du wirst das für mich tun, Narraboth. Du weisst, dass du das für mich tun wirst. Und morgen früh werde ich unter den Muss'linschleiern dir einen Blick zuwerfen, Narraboth, ich werde dich ansehn, kann sein, ich werde dir zulächeln. Sieh mich an, Narraboth, sieh mich an. Ah! wie gut du weisst, dass du tun wirst, um was ich dich bitte! Wie du es weisst! (*stark*) Ich weiss, du wirst das tun.

NARRABOTH

(*gibt den Soldaten ein Zeichen*)

Lasst den Propheten herauskommen. Die Prinzessin Salome wünscht ihn zu sehen.

SALOME

Ah!

(*Der Prophet kommt aus der Cisterne. Salome, in seinen Anblick versunken, weicht langsam vor ihm zurück.*)

JOCHANAAN

Wo ist er, dessen Sündenbecher jetzt voll ist? Wo ist er, der eines Tages im Angesicht alles Volkes in einem Silbermantel sterben wird? Heisst ihn herkommen, auf dass er die Stimme Dessen höre, der in den Wüsten und in den Häusern der Könige gekündet hat.

SALOME

Von wem spricht er?

FIRST SOLDIER

No, my Princess, he is quite young.

VOICE OF JOKANAAN

Don't rejoice, oh land of Palestine, that the rod of him who did smite thee is broken now. For from the sea of the serpent, soon a basilisk shall come and it shall grow and devour thy children.

SALOME

How strange his voice is! I wish that I could speak with him.

SECOND SOLDIER

My Princess, the Tetrarch ordered us to keep all people from him. Even the high Priest is forbidden to approach him.

SALOME

I desire to speak with this Prophet.

SECOND SOLDIER

It is impossible, my Princess.

SALOME (*still more excited*)

I'll speak to this prophet.
Have this prophet brought forth.

SECOND SOLDIER

We do not dare, my Princess.

SALOME

(*approaching the cistern and looking down into it*)

How black it is down below. What a dreadful thing to be in so black a pit, cold and dismal . . . It is like a tomb.
(*to the soldiers*)
Did you not hear? Bring the prophet out here. I wish to see him!

FIRST SOLDIER

My Princess, we cannot do what you have asked of us.

SALOME (*seeing Narraboth*)

Ah!

PAGE

Oh, I am afraid! I know something terrible will come.

SALOME

(*going up to Narraboth, speaking softly but animatedly*)

You will do this for me, Narraboth, won't you? You know I've always been kind to you. You will do this thing for me. I would but have a look at this strange and wondrous prophet. The Tetrarch has been talking so much about him. I think that he is afraid of him.

NARRABOTH

The Tetrarch has given out an order forbidding any man to remove the cover of this well.

SALOME

You will do this for me, Narraboth.
(*quickly*)
And tomorrow, when I pass in my litter through the gateway where the idol sellers sit, when I see you, I shall drop a little flower, for you I shall drop it, a tiny yellow flower.

NARRABOTH

My Princess, I cannot, I cannot!

SALOME (*precisely*)

You will do this for me, Narraboth, you know you will do what I asked of you. And tomorrow morning from behind my veils of muslin I shall look at you. Narraboth, I will look at you, maybe that I will smile at you. Look at me, Narraboth, look at me. Ah, how well you know that you'll do anything I ask you. How well you know! I know that you will do it!

NARABOTH

(*making a sign to the soldiers*)

Open the well for Jokanaan: The Princess Salome would speak with him!

SALOME

Ah!

(*The prophet comes out of the cistern. Salome looks at him and steps slowly back.*)

JOKANAAN

Where is he, who has sinned before the Almighty? Where is he who shall be chastened in front of all of the people? And with his power, God shall strike him down. Let him come forward. For he shall hear the voice of righteousness. The voice that crieth into the houses of kings and in the wilderness.

SALOME

Of whom does he speak?

NARRABOTH

Niemand kann es sagen, Prinzessin.

JOCHANAAN

Wo ist sie, die sich hingab der Lust ihrer Augen, die gestanden hat vor buntgemalten Männerbildern und Gesandte ins Land der Chaldäer schickte?

SALOME (*tonlos*)

Er spricht von meiner Mutter.

NARRABOTH (*heftig*)

Nein, nein Prinzessin.

SALOME (*matt*)

Ja, er spricht von meiner Mutter.

JOCHANAAN

Wo ist sie, die den Hauptleuten Assyriens sich gab? Wo ist sie, die sich den jungen Männern der Aegypter gegeben hat, die in feinem Leinen und Hyazinthgesteinen prangen, deren Schilde von Gold sind und die Leiber wie von Riesen? Geht, heisst sie aufstehn von dem Bett ihrer Greuel, vom Bett ihrer Blutschande; auf dass sie die Worte Dessen vernehme, der dem Herrn die Wege bereitet, und ihre Missetaten bereue. Und wenn sie gleich nicht bereut, heisst sie herkommen, denn die Geissel des Herrn ist in seiner Hand.

SALOME

Er ist schrecklich. Er ist wirklich schrecklich.

NARRABOTH

Bleibt nicht hier, Prinzessin, ich bitte Euch!

SALOME

Seine Augen sind von allem das Schrecklichste. Sie sind wie die schwarzen Höhlen, wo die Drachen hausen! Sie sind wie schwarze Seen, aus denen irres Mondlicht flackert. Glaubt ihr, dass er noch einmal sprechen wird?

NARRABOTH (*immer aufgeregter*)

Bleibt nicht hier, Prinzessin. Ich bitte Euch, bleibt nicht hier.

SALOME

Wie abgezehrt er ist! Er ist wie ein Bildnis aus Elfenbein. Gewiss ist er keusch wie der Mond. Sein Fleisch muss sehr kühl sein, kühl wie Elfenbein. Ich möchte ihn näher besehn.

NARRABOTH

Nein, nein, Prinzessin.

SALOME

Ich muss ihn näher besehn.

NARRABOTH

Prinzessin! Prinzessin!

JOCHANAAN

Wer ist dies Weib, das mich ansieht? Ich will ihre Augen nicht auf mir haben. Warum sieht sie mich so an mit ihren Goldaugen unter den gleissenden Lidern? Ich weiss nicht, wer sie ist. Ich will nicht wissen, wer sie ist. Heisst sie gehn! Zu ihr will ich nicht sprechen.

SALOME

Ich bin Salome, die Tochter der Herodias. Prinzessin von Judäa.

JOCHANAAN

Zurück, Tochter Babylons! Komm dem Erwählten des Herrn nicht nahe! Deine Mutter hat die Erde erfüllt mit dem Wein ihrer Lüste, und das Unmass ihrer Sünden schreit zu Gott.

SALOME

Sprich mehr, Jochanaan, deine Stimme ist wie Musik in meinen Ohren.

NARRABOTH

Prinzessin! Prinzessin! Prinzessin!

SALOME

Sprich mehr! Sprich mehr, Jochanaan, und sag' mir, was ich tun soll?

JOCHANAAN

Tochter Sodoms, komm mir nicht nahe! Vielmehr bedecke dein Gesicht mit einem Schleier, streue Asche auf deinen Kopf, mach dich auf in die Wüste und suche des Menschen Sohn.

SALOME

Wer ist das, des Menschen Sohn? Ist er so schön wie du, Jochanaan?

JOCHANAAN

Weiche von mir; Ich höre die Flügel des Todesengels im Palaste rauschen.

SALOME

Jochanaan!

NARRABOTH

Prinzessin, ich flehe, geh hinein!

NARRABOTH

No one can be certain, my Princess.

JOKANAAN

Where is she, who succumbed to the lust of her evil eyes, having seen on the walls the painted images of the Assyrians; whose ambassadors went into Babylon before her?

SALOME (*faintly*)

He speaks about my mother.

NARRABOTH (*violently*)

No, no, my Princess.

SALOME (*afflicted*)

Yes, he speaks about my mother.

JOKANAAN

Where is she, whom the Captains of Assyria possessed? Where is she who hath given herself to the young men of Egypt; they are clothed in linen and helmets made of silver, and their shields are of gold, and their bodies are mighty. Go, bid her rise now from her bed of incest, her bed of abominations, so that she may hear the words of warning from the one whom Jehovah hath chosen; and let her now repent of her sins. And if she does not repent, bid her come forward, for the rod of the Lord is in his hand.

SALOME

He is terrible! He is truly terrible.

NARRABOTH

Do not stay here, Princess, I beg of you!

SALOME

It's his eyes above all that are terrible. They're black as the caves of Egypt where the dragons make their lair! His eyes are like lakes on which fantastic moonlight flickers. Think you that we shall hear him speak again?

NARRABOTH

(*more and more excited*)

Do not stay here, Princess, I beg of you, do not stay.

SALOME

How pale and wan he is. He is like a statue of ivory. I am sure he is chaste as the moon. His flesh is like ivory, cool as ivory. I would like to look closer at him.

NARRABOTH

No, no, my Princess!

SALOME

I must look closer at him.

NARRABOTH

O Princess, my Princess!

JOKANAAN

Who is this woman who looks at me? I will not have her eyes look upon me. Wherefore doth she look at me with her eyes gleaming under her gilded eyelids? I know not who she is. I do not wish to know who she is. Bid her go! Because I will not speak to her.

SALOME

I am Salome, the daughter of Herodias, the Princess of Judaea.

JOKANAAN

Away! Daughter of Babylon! To the chosen of God approach not! Thy mother hath filled the earth with the lust of her body and the weight of her sinning cries to God.

SALOME

Say more, Jokanaan, your voice is to my ears celestial music.

NARRABOTH

O Princess, my Princess, my Princess.

SALOME

Say more, say more, Jokanaan, and tell me what to do.

JOKANAAN

Daughter of Sodom, come ye not near me! Go thou and cover up thy face with a veil. Scatter ashes upon thy head, get thee gone to the desert and seek out the Son of Man!

SALOME

Who is he, the Son of Man? Is he as fair as you, Jokanaan?

JOKANAAN

Out of my sight! I hear the wings of the Angel of Death, in the palace courtyard.

SALOME

Jokanaan!

NARRABOTH

My Princess, I beg you go within!

SALOME

Jochanaan! Ich bin verliebt in deinen Leib, Jochanaan! Dein Leib ist weiss wie die Lilien auf einem Felde, von der Sichel nie berührt. Dein Leib ist weiss wie der Schnee auf den Bergen Judäas. Die Rosen im Garten von Arabiens Königin sind nicht so weiss wie dein Leib, nicht die Rosen im Garten der Königin, nicht die Füsse der Dämmerung auf den Blättern, nicht die Brüste des Mondes auf dem Meere, nichts in der Welt ist so weiss wie dein Leib. Lass mich ihn berühren, deinen Leib!

JOCHANAAN

Zurück, Tochter Babylons! Durch das Weib kam das Uebel in die Welt. Sprich nicht zu mir. Ich will dich nicht anhör'n! Ich höre nur auf die Stimme des Herrn, meines Gottes.

SALOME

Dein Leib ist grauenvoll. Er ist wie der Leib eines Aussätzigen. Er ist wie eine getünchte Wand, wo Nattern gekrochen sind; wie eine getünchte Wand, wo die Skorpione ihr Nest gebaut. Er ist wie ein übertünchtes Grab voll widerlicher Dinge. Er ist grässlich, dein Leib ist grässlich. In dein Haar bin ich verliebt, Jochanaan. Dein Haar ist wie Weintrauben, wie Büschel schwarzer Trauben, an den Weinstöcken Edoms. Dein Haar ist wie die Cedern, die grossen Cedern vom Libanon, die den Löwen und Räubern Schatten spenden. Die langen schwarzen Nächte, wenn der Mond sich verbirgt, wenn die Sterne bangen, sind nicht so schwarz wie dein Haar. Des Waldes Schweigen. Nichts in der Welt ist so schwarz wie dein Haar. Lass mich es berühren, dein Haar!

JOCHANAAN

Zurück, Tochter Sodoms! Berühre mich nicht! Entweihe nicht den Tempel des Herrn, meines Gottes!

SALOME

Dein Haar ist grässlich! Es starrt von Staub und Unrat. Es ist wie eine Dornenkrone auf deinen Kopf gesetzt. Es ist wie ein Schlangenknoten gewickelt um deinen Hals. Ich liebe dein Haar nicht. (*mit höchster Leidenschaft*) Deinen Mund begehre ich, Jochanaan. Dein Mund ist wie ein Scharlachband an einem Turm von Elfenbein. Er ist wie ein Granatapfel, von einem Silbermesser zerteilt. Die Granatapfelblüten in den Gärten von Tyrus, glüh'nder als Rosen, sind nicht so rot. Die roten Fanfaren der Trompeten, die das Nah'n von Kön'gen künden und vor denen der Feind erzittert, sind nicht so rot, wie dein roter Mund. Dein Mund ist röter als die Füsse der Männer, die den Wein stampfen in der Kelter. Er ist röter als die Füsse der Tauben, die in den Tempeln wohnen. Dein Mund ist wie ein Korallenzweig in der Dämm'rung des Meer's, wie der Purpur in den Gruben von Moab, der Purpur der Könige. (*ausser sich*)

Nichts in der Welt ist so rot wie dein Mund. Lass mich ihn küssen, deinen Mund.

JOCHANAAN

(*leise, in tonlosem Schauder*)

Niemals, Tochter Babylons, Tochter Sodoms! Niemals!

SALOME

Ich will deinen Mund küssen, Jochanaan. Ich will deinen Mund küssen.

NARRABOTH

(*in höchster Angst und Verzweiflung*)

Prinzessin, Prinzessin, die wie ein Garten von Myrrhen ist, die die Taube aller Tauben ist, sieh diesen Mann nicht an. Sprich nicht solche Worte zu ihm. Ich kann es nicht ertragen.

SALOME

Ich will deinen Mund küssen, Jochanaan. Ich will deinen Mund küssen,

(*Narraboth ersticht sich und fällt tot zwischen Salome und Jochanaan.*)

SALOME

Lass mich deinen Mund küssen, Jochanaan!

JOCHANAAN

Wird dir nicht bange, Tochter der Herodias?

SALOME

Lass mich deinen Mund küssen, Jochanaan!

SALOME

Jokanaan! I am amorous of your body! Jokanaan! It is as white and as fragrant as are the lilies of the field at break of day. Your body's white as the snows on the hills of Judaea. The roses in gardens of the Queen of Arabia are not so white as your body. Nor the garden of spices of the Queen of Tyre. Nor the feet of the dawn that light on the flowers, nor the breast of the moon on the breast of the ocean; naught in the world is so white as you are. Let me touch your body, touch your flesh.

JOKANAAN

Away, Daughter of Babylon! It was woman who brought evil into the world. Bridle your tongue. I will never heed you. All I will heed is the voice of the Lord, God Almighty.

SALOME

Your flesh is horrible. It looks like the flesh of a leper unclean. Is it not like a bespattered wall, all crawling with snakes and toads, like a bespattered wall where scorpions have made their nest? It is like an ancient ruined tomb that's full of loathsome vermin. It is ghastly; your body is ghastly. It's your hair that I adore, Jokanaan. Your hair is like ripe, black grapes; like dusky purple grapes from the vineyards of Edom. Your hair is like the cedars, the cedars of Lebanon, which the lions and robbers take shelter under . . .
The nights of endless silence when the moon will not shine and the stars show faintly are not so black as your hair. The forest stillness. . . Naught in the world is so black as your hair. Suffer me to fondle your hair.

JOKANAAN

Away! Daughter of Sodom! And touch me not! Profane ye not the temple of the Lord, God Almighty.

SALOME

Your hair is ghastly! It's stiff with dirt and mire. It's like a crown of thorns put on your head in jest. It's like a nest of serpents; in coils they writhe about your neck. I love not your black hair. It's your mouth that I desire, Jokanaan. It is your mouth that I desire, Jokanaan. Your mouth is like a band of scarlet on a tower of ivory. It is like a pomegranate that with a silver knife has been cut. Ah, the pomegranate flowers in the garden of Tyre though redder than Roses are not so red. The blaze of the trumpets that herald the approach of kings in war time, and that fill all the foe with terror, are not so red as your crimson mouth. Your mouth is redder than the feet of the men who tread the wine, stamping in the wine-press. It is redder than the feet of the doves haunting all the temples. Your mouth is like a coral branch in the twilight of the sea: like vermilion in the mines of far Moab, the color of royalty. (*ecstatically*. Naught in the world is so red as your mouth. Ah, let me kiss it, kiss your mouth.

JOKANAAN

(*softly, silently shuddering*)

Never! Daughter of Babylon! Daughter of Sodom! Never!

SALOME

Let me kiss your mouth, your mouth Jokanaan! I'll kiss your mouth, Jokanaan!

NARRABOTH

(*in great fear and despair*)

My Princess, my Princess, you are a garden of sweetest myrrh, you are fairer than the dove of doves. Do not look at him. Do not speak such words to him. I cannot bear to hear them!

SALOME

Let me kiss your mouth, your mouth, Jokanaan.
Let me kiss your mouth, Jokanaan.

(*Narraboth kills himself and falls between Salome and Jokanaan.*)

SALOME

Let me kiss your mouth, Jokanaan.

JOKANAAN

Art thou not frightened, Daughter of Herodias?

SALOME

Let me kiss your mouth, your mouth, Jokanaan!

JOCHANAAN

Tochter der Unzucht, es lebt nur Einer,
der dich retten kann. Geh', such'
ihn.

(*mit grösster Wärme*)

Such' ihn. Er ist in einem Nachen auf
dem See von Galiläa und redet zu
seinen Jüngern.

Knie nieder am Ufer des Sees, ruf ihn
an und rufe ihn beim Namen. Wenn
er zu dir kommt, und er kommt zu
allen, die ihn rufen, dann bücke dich
zu seinen Füssen, dass er dir deine
Sünden vergebe.

SALOME (*wie verzweifelt*)

Lass mich deinen Mund küssen, Jochanaan!

JOCHANAAN

Sei verflucht, Tochter der blutschän-
derischen Mutter, sei verflucht!

SALOME

Lass mich deinen Mund küssen, Jochanaan!

JOCHANAAN

Ich will dich nicht ansehn. Du bist,
verflucht, Salome. Du bist verflucht.

(*Er geht wieder in die Cisterne hinab.
Herodes, Herodias treten mit Gefolge
ein.*)

HERODES

Wo ist Salome? Wo ist die Prinzessin?
Warum kam sie nicht wieder zum
Bankett wie ich ihr befohlen hatte?
Ah! Da ist sie!

HERODIAS

Du sollst sie nicht ansehn. Fortwährend
siehst du sie an!

HERODES

Wie der Mond heute nacht aussieht!
Ist es nicht ein seltsames Bild? Es
sieht aus wie ein wahnwitziges Weib,
das überall nach Buhlen sucht . . . wie
ein betrunkenes Weib das durch Wol-
ken taumelt.

HERODIAS

Nein, der Mond ist wie der Mond, das
ist alles. Wir wollen hineingehn.

HERODES

Ich will hier bleiben. Manassah, leg
Teppiche hierher! Zündet Fackeln

an! Ich will noch Wein mit meinen
Gästen trinken! Ah! Ich bin ausge-
glitten. Ich bin in Blut getreten, **das**
ist ein böses Zeichen. Warum ist hier
Blut? Und dieser Tote? Wer ist dieser Tote hier? Wer ist dieser Tote?
Ich will ihn nicht sehn.

ERSTER SOLDAT

Es ist unser Hauptmann, Herr.

HERODES

Ich erliess keinen Befehl, dass er getötet werde.

ERSTER SOLDAT

Er hat sich selbst getötet, Herr.

HERODES

Das scheint mir seltsam. Der junge
Syrier, er war sehr schön. Ich erin-
nere mich, ich sah seine schmachten-
den Augen, wenn er Salome ansah.
Fort mit ihm.

(*Sie tragen den Leichnam weg.*)

Es ist kalt hier. Es weht ein Wind.
Weht nicht ein Wind?

HERODIAS (*trocken*)

Nein, es weht kein Wind.

HERODES

Ich sage euch, es weht ein Wind. Und
in der Luft höre ich etwas wie **das**
Rauschen von mächtigen Flügeln.
Hört ihr es nicht?

HERODIAS

Ich höre nichts.

HERODES

Jetzt höre ich es nicht mehr. Aber ich
habe es gehört, es war das Wehn **des**
Windes. Es ist vorüber. Horch! Hört
ihr es nicht? Das Rauschen von
mächt'gen Flügeln.

HERODIAS

Du bist krank, wir wollen hineingehn.

HERODES

Ich bin nicht krank. Aber deine Tochter ist krank zu Tode. Niemals hab
ich sie so blass gesehn.

HERODIAS

Ich habe dir gesagt, du sollst **sie nicht**
ansehn.

JOKANAAN

Daughter of adultery, there is but one man who can save thy soul. Go, seek Him.

(*with great warmth*)

Seek Him. He waiteth in his boat there on the sea of Galilaea and speaketh with his disciples.

(*with great solemnity*)

Kneel down there on the shore of the sea and call to him. And call to Him by his holy name. And when He cometh, and He comes to everyone who calls him, then bow thyself and beg for mercy. He will cleanse thee and He will forgive thee.

SALOME (*desperately*)

Let me kiss your mouth, Jokanaan, Jokanaan!

JOKANAAN

Be thou curst, daughter of an incestuous mother, curst be thou!

SALOME

Let me kiss your mouth, kiss it, Jokanaan.

JOKANAAN

I will not see thee. Thou art accursed. Salome. Thou art accursed.

(*He goes down into the cistern. Herod and Herodias enter with their entourage.*)

HEROD

Where is Salome? Where is the Princess? And why did she not return to the banquet as I commanded her? Ah! There she is!

HERODIAS

You must not look at her. You're always looking at her.

HEROD

See how strange the moon looks. Has she not the strangest look? She is like a wild crazy woman who seeks for lovers everywhere. She's like a drunken woman who is reeling through the clouds.

HERODIAS

No; the moon is like the moon.
That is all. Let's return to the banquet.

HEROD

I will not go back! Manasseh, lay carpets down for us!

Light the torches! Pour out some wine and tell my guests to join me. Ah, I have slipped on something. Ah, it was blood I slipped on. It is an evil omen . . . And why is there blood? And this body? Speak! Why is this body here? Who is this dead man? I do not want to see him.

FIRST SOLDIER

It is our captain, sire.

HEROD

I had not given an order that this man be killed.

FIRST SOLDIER

He has killed himself, sire.

HEROD

That seems quite strange. . . This young Syrian . . . was very fair. I remember now I saw his langorous eyes watching Salome with longing. Off with him.

(*They remove the body.*)

It is cold here. The wind is cold. . .
Is there a wind?

HERODIAS (*dryly*)

No, there is no wind.

HEROD

I say again. . . There is a wind, and in the air. . . I hear something, like enormous wings are beating. . . . Do you not hear?

HERODIAS

I hear nothing.

HEROD

Now I hear it no more, but I heard something blowing. It was the sound of winds. Now it is over. . . Now!. . . Now do you hear?. . . Enormous wings are beating. . .

HERODIAS

You are sick. Let's return to the palace.

HEROD

I am not sick. It is your daughter who is sick to death. . . Never have I seen her pale as this.

HERODIAS

I have already said that you must not look at her!

HERODES

Schenkt mir Wein ein.

(*Es wird Wein gebracht.*)

Salome, komm, trink Wein mit mir, einen köstlichen Wein. Cäsar selbst hat ihn mir geschickt Tauche deine kleinen roten Lippen hinein, deine kleinen roten Lippen, dann will ich den Becher leeren.

SALOME

Ich bin nicht durstig, Tetrarch.

HERODES

Hörst du, wie sie mir antwortet, diese deine Tochter?

HERODIAS

Sie hat recht. Warum starrst du sie immer an?

HERODES

Bringt reife Früchte.

(*Es werden Früchte gebracht.*)

Salome, komm, iss mit mir von diesen Früchten. Den Abdruck deiner kleinen, weissen Zähne in einer Frucht seh' ich so gern. Beiss nur ein wenig ab, nur ein wenig von dieser Frucht, dann will ich essen, was übrig ist.

SALOME

Ich bin nicht hungrig, Tetrarch.

HERODES (*zu Herodias*)

Du siehst, wie du diese deine Tochter erzogen hast!

HERODIAS

Meine Tochter und ich stammen aus königlichem Blut. Dein Vater war Kameeltreiber, dein Vater war ein Dieb und ein Räuber obendrein.

HERODES

Salome, komm, setz dich zu mir. Du sollst auf dem Tron deiner Mutter sitzen.

SALOME

Ich bin nicht müde, Tetrarch.

HERODIAS

Du siehst, wie sie dich achtet.

HERODES

Bringt mir--was wünsche ich denn? Ich habe es vergessen. Ah! Ah! Ich erinnre mich.

DIE STIMME DES JOCHANAAN

Siehe, die Zeit ist gekommen, der Tag, von dem ich sprach, ist da.

HERODIAS

Heiss' ihn schweigen! Dieser Mensch beschimpft mich!

HERODES

Er hat nichts gegen dich gesagt. Ueberdies ist er ein sehr grosser Prophet.

HERODIAS

Ich glaube nicht an Propheten. Aber du, du hast Angst vor ihm.

HERODES

Ich habe vor niemandem Angst.

HERODIAS

Ich sage dir, du hast Angst vor ihm. Warum lieferst du ihn nicht den Juden aus, die seit Monaten nach ihm schreien?

ERSTER JUDE

Wahrhaftig, Herr, es wäre besser, ihn in unsre Hände zu geben!

HERODES

Genug davon! Ich werde ihn nicht in eure Hände geben. Er ist ein heiliger Mann. Er ist ein Mann, der Gott geschaut hat.

ERSTER JUDE

Das kann nicht sein. Seit dem Propheten Elias hat niemand Gott gesehn. Er war der letzte, der Gott von Angesicht geschaut. In unsren Tagen zeigt sich Gott nicht. Gott verbirgt sich. Darum ist grosses Uebel über das Land gekommen, grosses Uebel.

ZWEITER JUDE

In Wahrheit weiss niemand, ob Elias in der Tat Gott gesehen hat. Möglicherweise war es nur der Schatten Gottes, was er sah.

DRITTER JUDE

Gott ist zu keiner Zeit verborgen. Er zeigt sich zu allen Zeiten und an allen Orten. Gott ist im schlimmen ebenso wie im guten.

VIERTER JUDE

Du solltest das nicht sagen, es ist eine sehr gefährliche Lehre aus Alexandria. Und die Griechen sind Heiden.

HEROD

Pour out wine for me. . .

(*Wine is brought.*)

Salome, come drink wine with me. This is exquisite wine. Wine that Caesar sent me himself. Touch it with your little rosy red lips; Ah, such little rosy red lips. Then I will drain the goblet.

SALOME

I am not thirsty, Tetrarch.

HEROD

Hear how she answers me, this your daughter!

HERODIAS

She is right. Why are you staring at her like that?

HEROD

Bring me ripe mangoes. . .

(*Fruit is brought.*)

Salome, come eat with me luscious ripe mangoes. . . . I'd love to see the imprint of your teeth in this luscious fruit. Taste it for me. Take but one little bite, just a small bite of this sweet mango. Then I shall eat what is left for me.

SALOME

I am not hungry, Tetrarch.

HEROD (*to Herodias*)

You see how you have brought up this daughter of yours. You see!

HERODIAS

My daughter and I, both of us are of royal blood. Your father was a camel driver. Your father was a thief and a robber and furthermore. . . .

HEROD

Salome, come sit next to me. I'll give you the throne of your mother to sit upon. . . .

SALOME

I am not tired, Tetrarch.

HERODIAS

You see what she thinks of you.

HEROD

Bring me . . . what is it I want? . . . It seems I have forgotten. . . . Ah! . . . Ah! . . . I remember now . . .

VOICE OF JOKANAAN

Now the time is upon us, the hour of which I spoke is come.

HERODIAS

Make him silent. For this man insults me.

HEROD

He has not even mentioned you. And besides he's a seer and a prophet.

HERODIAS

I don't believe in prophets. As for you, you're afraid of him.

HEROD

I . . . I am not afraid of him.

HERODIAS

I tell you that you are afraid of him. Why not deliver him to the Hebrews there; he's the one for whom they have been screaming.

FIRST JEW

In truth, my lord, it were much better to deliver him into our hands.

HEROD

Enough of this! I told you I will not give him into your hands. He is a holy man. This man has seen the Lord, the Almighty.

FIRST JEW

That cannot be. Since the great prophet Elias no one has seen our Lord. He was the last man who looked on God face to face. And in these later days the Lord has turned his face away. Therefore, are days of evil fallen upon our nation, days of evil.

SECOND JEW

But who can be certain that Elias really saw the Lord our God. Is it not likely that it was but the Lord's reflection that he saw.

THIRD JEW

God never hides from those who seek him. He showeth his mighty power in all times and places. God is in evil just as he is in goodness.

FOURTH JEW

Why do you speak such falsehood? Forsooth that is false and dangerous doctrine from Alexandria. And the Greeks are pagans.

FUENFTER JUDE

Niemand kann sagen, wie Gott wirkt. Seine Wege sind sehr dunkel. Wir können nur unser Haupt unter seinen Willen beugen, denn Gott ist sehr stark.

ERSTER JUDE

Du sagst die Wahrheit. Fürwahr, Gott ist furchtbar. Aber was diesen Menschen angeht, der hat Gott nie gesehn. Seit dem Propheten Elias hat niemand Gott gesehn. Er war der letzte, der Gott von Angesicht zu Angesicht geschaut. In unsren Tagen zeigt sich Gott nicht. Gott verbirgt sich. Darum ist grosses Uebel über das Land gekommen.

HERODIAS (*zu Herodes, heftig*)

Heiss' sie schweigen, sie langweilen mich.

HERODES

Doch hab' ich davon sprechen hören, Jochanaan sei in Wahrheit euer Prophet Elias.

ERSTER JUDE

Das kann nicht sein. Seit den Tagen des Propheten Elias sind mehr als dreihundert Jahre vergangen.

ERSTER NAZARENER

Mir ist sicher, dass er der Prophet Elias ist.

ERSTER JUDE

Das kann nicht sein. Seit den Tagen des Propheten Elias sind mehr als dreihundert Jahre vergangen.

DIE ANDEREN JUDEN

Keineswegs, er ist nicht der Prophet Elias.

HERODIAS

Heiss' sie schweigen!

DIE STIMME DES JOCHANAAN

Siehe, der Tag ist nahe, der Tag des Herrn, und ich höre auf den Bergen die Schritte Dessen, der sein wird der Erlöser der Welt.

HERODES

Was soll das heissen, der Erlöser der Welt?

ERSTER NAZARENER (*emphatisch*)

Der Messias ist gekommen.

ERSTER JUDE (*schreiend*)

Der Messias ist nicht gekommen.

ERSTER NAZARENER

Er ist gekommen, und allenthalben tut er Wunder. Bei einer Hochzeit in Galiläa hat er Wasser in Wein verwandelt. Er heilte zwei Aussätzige von Capernaum.

ZWEITER NAZARENER

Durch blosses Berühren!

ERSTER NAZARENER

Er hat auch Blinde geheilt. Man hat ihn auf einem Berge im Gespräch mit Engeln gesehn!

HERODIAS

Oho! Ich glaube nicht an Wunder, ich habe ihrer zu viele gesehn!

ERSTER NAZARENER

Die Tochter des Jairus hat er von den Toten erweckt.

HERODES (*erschreckt*)

Wie, er erweckt die Toten?

ERSTER UND ZWEITER NAZARENER

Jawohl. Er erweckt die Toten.

HERODES

Ich verbiete ihm, das zu tun. Es wäre schrecklich, wenn die Toten wiederkämen! Wo ist der Mann zur Zeit?

ERSTER NAZARENER

Herr, er ist überall, aber es ist schwer, ihn zu finden.

HERODES

Der Mann muss gefunden werden.

ZWEITER NAZARENER

Es heisst, in Samaria weile er jetzt.

ERSTER NAZARENER

Vor ein paar Tagen verliess er Samaria, ich glaube, im Augenblick ist er in der Nähe von Jerusalem.

FIFTH JEW

No man can tell us how God works, for his ways are dark and hidden. We can but bow our heads before his mighty power, for God is very strong.

FIRST JEW

Now you speak truly. Oh yes, God is fearsome. But of this man I am quite certain: He hath never seen God. Since the prophet Elias no man hath seen the Lord.

He was the last one to stand before our Lord and see him face to face. And in these latter days the Lord has turned his face away, turned his face away. Therefore are days of evil fallen upon our nation.

HERODIAS

(to Herod, bursting out)

Make them be silent, they bore me to death.

HEROD

But I have heard it sometimes said that Jokanaan himself is . . . is your prophet Elias.

FIRST JEW

That cannot be, since the days of the prophet Elias more than three hundred years have elapsed.

FIRST NAZARENE

I am sure that he is the prophet Elias.

FIRST JEW

That cannot be. Since the days of the prophet Elias more than three hundred years are gone.

THE OTHER JEWS

Not at all. He is not the prophet Elias.

HERODIAS

Bid them be silent!

VOICE OF JOKANAAN

Low now, the day is dawning, the day of the Lord. And I hear upon the mountains the glorious footsteps of Him Who is the Redeemer of man.

HEROD

What does that mean, "the Redeemer of man"?

FIRST NAZARENE (emphatically)

The Messiah now is with us!

FIRST JEW (crying)

The Messiah is not yet with us!

FIRST NAZARENE

Yes, he is coming I've heard the stories. He works miracles. For, at a wedding in Galilea, he was there and made wine from water. Two lepers were healed by him in Capernaum.

SECOND NAZARENE

He touched them and healed them.

FIRST NAZARENE

The lame and blind he has healed. Some have seen him on the mountain as he talks to the angels of heaven.

HERODIAS

Ho, ho! I don't believe in miracles because too often I've seen they are false.

FIRST NAZARENE

The daughter of Jairus, he has raised her up from the dead.

HEROD (frightened)

What! Even raised the dead?

FIRST AND SECOND NAZARENE

Yea, sire, He can raise the dead.

HEROD

I forbid Him to raise the dead. It would be dreadful if the dead came back to haunt us! Where can this man be found?

FIRST NAZARENE

Sire, He is everywhere but no one can tell where to find Him.

HEROD

This man must be found at once.

SECOND NAZARENE

They say that in Samaria He may be found.

FIRST NAZARENE

He hath deserted Samaria as I heard it, and some people say that He's close by in the mountains near Jerusalem.

HERODES

So hört: Ich verbiete ihm die Toten zu erwecken! Es müsste schrecklich sein, wenn die Toten wiederkämen!

DIE STIMME DES JOCHANAAN

O über dieses geile Weib, die Tochter Babylons. So spricht der Herr, unser Gott: Eine Menge Menschen wird sich gegen sie sammeln, und sie werden Steine nehmen und sie steinigen!

HERODIAS (*wütend*)

Befiehl ihm, er soll schweigen! Wahrhaftig, es ist schändlich!

DIE STIMME DES JOCHANAAN

Die Kriegshauptleute werden sie mit ihren Schwertern durchbohren, sie werden sie mit ihren Schilden zermalmen!

HERODIAS

Er soll schweigen!

DIE STIMME JOCHANAAN

Es ist so, dass ich alle Verruchtheit austilgen werde, dass ich alle Weiber lehren werde, nicht auf den Wegen ihrer Greuel zu wandeln!

HERODIAS

Du hörst, was er gegen mich sagt, du duldest es, dass er die schmähe, die dein Weib ist.

HERODES

Er hat deinen Namen nicht genannt.

DIE STIMME DES JOCHANAAN

(*sehr feierlich*)

Es kommt ein Tag, da wird die Sonne finster werden wie ein schwarzes Tuch. Und der Mond wird werden wie Blut, und die Sterne des Himmels werden zur Erde fallen wie unreife Feigen vom Feigenbaum. Es kommt ein Tag, wo die Kön'ge der Erde erzittern.

HERODIAS

Ha ha! Dieser Prophet schwatzt wie ein Betrunkener. Aber ich kann den Klang seiner Stimme nicht ertragen, ich hasse seine Stimme. Befiehl ihm, er soll schweigen.

HERODES

Tanz für mich, Salome.

HERODIAS (*heftig*)

Ich will nicht haben, dass sie tanzt.

SALOME (*ruhig*)

Ich habe keine Lust zu tanzen, Tetrarch.

HERODES

Salome, Tochter der Herodias, tanz für mich!

SALOME

Ich will nicht tanzen, Tetrarch.

HERODIAS

Du siehst, wie sie dir gehorcht.

HERODES

Salome, Salome, tanz für mich, ich bitte dich. Ich bin traurig heute nacht, drum tanz für mich. Salome, tanz für mich! Wenn du für mich tanzest, kannst du von mir begehren, was du willst. Ich werde es dir geben.

DIE STIMME DES JOCHANAAN

Er wird auf seinem Trone sitzen, er wird gekleidet sein in Scharlach und Purpur. Und der Engel des Herrn wird ihn darniederschlagen. Er wird von den Würmern gefressen werden.

SALOME (*aufstehend*)

Willst du mir wirklich alles geben, was ich von dir begehre, Tetrarch?

HERODIAS

Tanze nicht, meine Tochter.

HERODES

Alles, was du von mir begehren wirst, und wär's die Hälfte meines Königreichs.

SALOME

Du schwörst es, Tetrarch?

HERODES

Ich schwör' es, Salome.

SALOME

Wobei willst du das beschwören, Tetrarch?

HERODES

Bei meinem Leben, bei meiner Krone, bei meinen Göttern. O Salome, Salome, tanz für mich!

HERODIAS

Tanze nicht, meine Tochter!

HEROD

Here now, I forbid that the dead should be awakened. It would be terrible if the dead came back to haunt us!

VOICE OF JOKANAAN

Oh curst be this wanton one! The daughter of Babylon thus saith the Lord, our God. And then a crowd of men shall come and shall revile her name, and they shall heap filth upon her, and cast stones at her!

HERODIAS (*furiously*)

Command him to be silent! You hear that: this is infamous . . .

VOICE OF JOKANAAN

The captains and the men-at-arms shall strike her down with their weapons, and then beneath their shields of brass she shall die at last!

HERODIAS

Make him be silent!

VOICE OF JOKANAAN

I'll stamp out from the face of the earth such abominations. And, thus shall I teach the wanton women not to be following her path to damnation!

HERODIAS

You hear what he says against me? You allow this? To insult her who is your wife?

HEROD

Not once did he mention you by name!

VOICE OF JOKANAAN
(*very solemnly*)

The day will come, that day of wrath the earth shall tremble and the sun turn black, and the moon turn crimson, like blood, and the stars of the heavens fall like a hail of fire! The mountains shall flame and the seas shall boil! And on that day all the crowns of the earth shall tremble.

HERODIAS

Ha, ha! Hear how this seer talks just like a drunken man . . . but I cannot stand to hear it, I can't stand it. I hate the sound of his voice. Command him to be silent!

HEROD

Dance for me, Salome.

HERODIAS (*violently*)

I do not want her to dance.

SALOME (*quietly*)

I have no desire to dance, Tetrarch.

HEROD

Salome, Daughter of Herodias, dance for me!

SALOME

I will not dance, Tetrarch.

HERODIAS

You see how she obeys you.

HEROD

Salome, Salome, dance for me, I beg of you. I am very sad tonight, so dance for me, Salome, dance for me. If you but dance now, then I will gladly grant you any desire. I'll give you all you ask for.

VOICE OF JOKANAAN

Upon his throne he shall be seated, and he shall wear his robe of scarlet and purple. And the angel of God shall strike him down with lightning and then the worms shall devour his body.

SALOME (*rising*)

But will you really give me anything that I ask of you, Tetrarch?

HERODIAS

Do not dance, my daughter.

HEROD

All, all that you shall ask I will give to you. I'll give you half of my whole kingdom.

SALOME

You swear to it, Tetrarch?

HEROD

I swear it, Salome.

SALOME

By what do you swear to do it, Tetrarch?

HEROD

By my own life's blood and by my kingdom. By all that's holy. O Salome, Salome, dance for me.

HERODIAS

Do not dance my daughter!

SALOME

Du hast einen Eid geschworen, Tetrarch.

HERODES

Ich habe einen Eid geschworen!

HERODIAS

Meine Tochter, tanze nicht!

HERODES

Und wär's die Hälfte meines Königreichs. Du wirst schön sein als Königin, unermesslich schön.

(erschauernd)

Ah! es ist kalt hier. Es weht ein eis'ger Wind und ich höre. Warum höre ich in der Luft dieses Rauschen von Flügeln? Ah! Es ist doch so, als ob ein ungeheurer, schwarzer Vogel über der Terrasse schwebte? Warum kann ich ihn nicht sehn, diesen Vogel? Dieses Rauschen ist schrecklich. Es ist ein schneidender Wind. Aber nein, er ist nicht kalt, er ist heiss. Giesst mir Wasser über die Hände, gebt mir Schnee zu essen, macht mir den Mantel los. Schnell, schnell, macht mir den Mantel los! Doch nein! Lasst ihn! Dieser Kranz drückt mich. Diese Rosen sind wie Feuer.

(Er reisst sich das Kranzgewinde ab und wirft es auf den Tisch.)

Ah! Jetzt kann ich atmen. Jetzt bin ich glücklich.

(matt)

Willst du für mich tanzen, Salome?

HERODIAS

Ich will nicht haben, dass sie tanze!

SALOME

Ich will für dich tanzen.

(Sklavinnen bringen Salben und die sieben Schleier und nehmen Salome die Sandalen ab.)

DIE STIMME DES JOCHANAAN

Wer ist Der, der von Edom kommt, wer ist Der, der von Bosra kommt, dessen Kleid mit Purpur gefärbt ist, der in der Schönheit seiner Gewänder leuchtet, der mächtig in seiner Grösse wandelt, warum ist dein Kleid mit Scharlach gefleckt?

HERODIAS

Wir wollen hineingehn. Die Stimme dieses Menschen macht mich wahnsinnig.

(immer heftiger)

Ich will nicht haben, dass mein Tochter tanzt, während er immer dazwischenschreit. Ich will nicht haben, dass sie tanzt, während du sie auf solche Art ansiehst. Mit einem Wort: ich will nicht haben, dass sie tanzt.

HERODES

Steh nicht auf, mein Weib, meine Königin. Es wird dir nichts helfen, ich gehe nicht hinein, bevor sie getanzt hat. Tanze, Salome, tanz für mich!

HERODIAS

Tanze nicht, meine Tochter!

SALOME

Ich bin bereit, Tetrarch.

(Die Musikanten beginnen einen wilden Tanz. Salome, zuerst noch bewegungslos, richtet sich hoch auf und gibt den Musikanten ein Zeichen, worauf der wilde Rhythmus sofort abgedämpft wird und in eine sanft wiegende Weise überleitet. Salome tanzt sodann den.

Tanz der sieben Schleier

(Sie scheint einen Augenblick zu ermatten, jetzt rafft sie sich wie neubeschwingt auf. Sie verweilt einen Augenblick in visionärer Haltung an der Cisterne, in der Jochanaan gefangen gehalten wird; dann stürzt sie vor und zu Herodes' Füssen.)

HERODES

Ah! Herrlich! Wundervoll, wundervoll!

(zu Herodias)

Siehst du, sie hat für mich getanzt, deine Tochter. Komm her, Salome, komm her, du sollst deinen Lohn haben. Ich will dich königlich belohnen. Ich will dir alles geben, was dein Herz begehrt. Was willst du haben? Sprich!

SALOME (süss)

Ich möchte, dass sie mir gleic in einer Silberschüssel . . .

HERODES (lachend)

In einer Silberschüssel — gewiss doch — in einer Silberschüssel. Sie ist reizend, nicht? Was ist's, das du in einer Silberschüssel haben möchtest, o süsse, schöne Salome, du, die schöner ist als alle Töchter Judäas? Was sollen sie dir in einer Silberschüssel bringen? Sag es mir! Was es auch sein mag, du sollst es erhalten. Meine Reichtümer gehören dir. Was ist es, das du haben möchtest. Salome?

SALOME

Remember the oath you've taken Tetrarch.

HEROD

I've taken an oath, I know it.

HERODIAS

My daughter, do not dance.

HEROD

I'll give you half of my whole kingdom! As a queen you'll be fairest of all, fairest queen of all. (*shivering*) Ah! It is cold here! There is an icy wind, and I hear . . . What's that sound I hear in the air? Wings of death now are beating! Ah! It seems as if . . . as if there were a bird, a great black monster hov'ring over us and waiting! But why, why can I not see it . . . this great monster? This wild beating is frightful! There is a cold freezing wind! . . . No, it's not . . . No, it's not cold, it is hot! Pour some water over my hot hands, give me snow! I'm choking. Tear loose my mantle, quick! Quick, quick, tear loose my mantle, quick! No, no, leave it! It's my wreath hurts me! Ah! These roses are like fire.

(*He tears the wreath from his head and throws it on the table.*)

Ah! Now I breathe . . . Now I am happy.

(*faintly*)

Will you not dance, Salome?

HERODIAS

I will forbid it! She must not dance.

SALOME

I'll dance for you, Tetrarch.

(*Slaves bring perfumes and the seven veils and take off Salome's sandals.*)

VOICE OF JOKANAAN

Who is He who from Edom cometh, who is He who from Bozra cometh, and whose raiment is colored with purple, He who is shining now with a holy glory? Who, mighty in His greatness, walketh. Wherefore is Thy raiment stained with Thy blood?

HERODIAS

Come, let us go inside! Let us go inside; the voice of that man maddens me.

(*more fiercely*)

I'll not allow it! I will not have her dance while he keeps screaming away like that! I will not have my daughter dance while you stare at her in such a fashion. And, in one word, I will not have my daughter dance.

HEROD

Do not rise, my wife. Do not rise, my Queen. For I am determined I will not go inside until she hath danced. Dance, Salome, dance for me!

HERODIAS

Do not dance, my daughter!

SALOME

Now I will dance, Tetrarch.

(*The musicians begin with a wild dance. Salome, at first, motionless, draws herself up and gives the musicians a sign upon which the wild rhythm is at once relaxed and a gentle rocking melody takes place. Salome then dances the* Dance of the Seven Veils.)

(*For a moment she seems exhausted, then rouses herself with renewed vigor. She halts an instant in visionary attitude near the cistern where Jokanaan is imprisoned, then falls forward at Herod's feet.*)

HEROD

Ah! Wondrous, wonderful, wonderful! Ah! You see, Salome has danced. Your fair daughter! Come here. Salome, come here. You will have your wishes granted. I'll give you all your heart's desire. I'll give you all you ask for, all your heart's desires. What will you have then? Speak!

SALOME (*sweetly*)

I would that they bring me in a silver vessel . . .

HEROD (*laughing*)

In a silver vessel! But surely in a silver vessel . . . She is charming, no? What would you have brought in a silver vessel for your pleasure? Oh sweetest, fairest Salome. You who are most fair of all the daughters of Judaea . . . What would you have brought you in a silver vessel, tell me? Tell me now! Whatever it may be, to you t'will be given. All my treasures belong to you. What is it, you will have from me, Salome?

SALOME (*steht auf, lächelnd*)
Den Kopf des Jochanaan.

HERODES (*fährt auf*)
Nein, nein!

HERODIAS
Ah! Das sagst du gut, meine Tochter.
Das sagst du gut!

HERODES
Nein, nein, Salome; das ist es nicht,
was du begehrst! Hör' nicht auf die
Stimme deiner Mutter. Sie gab dir
immer schlechten Rat. Achte nicht
auf sie.

SALOME
Ich achte nicht auf die Stimme meiner
Mutter. Zu meiner eignen Lust will
ich den Kopf des Jochanaan in einer
Silberschüssel haben. Du hast einen
Eid geschworen, Herodes. Du hast
einen Eid geschworen, vergiss das
nicht!

HERODES (*hastig*)
Ich weiss, ich habe einen Eid geschworen. Ich weiss es wohl. Bei meinen
Göttern habe ich es geschworen.
Aber ich beschwöre dich, Salome,
verlange etwas andres von mir. Verlange die Hälfte meines Königreichs.
Ich will sie dir geben. Aber verlange
nicht von mir, was deine Lippen
verlangten.

SALOME (*stark*)
Ich verlange von dir den Kopf des
Jochanaan!

HERODES
Nein, nein, ich will ihn dir nicht geben.

SALOME
Du hast einen Eid geschworen, Herodes.

HERODIAS
Ja, du hast einen. Eid geschworen. Alle
haben es gehört.

HERODES
Still, Weib, zu dir spreche ich nicht.

HERODIAS
Meine Tochter hat recht daran getan,
den Kopf des Jochanaan zu verlangen. Er hat mich mit Schimpf und
Schande bedeckt. Man kann sehn,
dass sie ihre Mutter liebt. Gib nicht
nach, meine Tochter, gibt nicht
nach! Er hat einen Eid geschworen.

HERODES
Still, sprich nicht zu mir! Salome, ich
beschwöre dich: Sei nicht trotzig!
Sieh, ich habe dich immer lieb gehabt. Kann sein, ich habe dich zu
lieb gehabt. Darum verlange das
nicht von mir. Der Kopf eines Mannes, der vom Rumpf getrennt ist, ist
ein übler Anblick. Hör', was ich sage!
Ich habe einen Smaragd. Er ist der
schönste Smaragd der ganzen Welt.
Den willst du haben, nicht wahr?
Verlang' ihn von mir, ich will ihn
dir geben, den schönsten Smaragd.

SALOME
Ich fordre den Kopf des Jochanaan!

HERODES
Du hörst nicht zu, du hörst nicht zu.
Lass mich zu dir reden, Salome!

SALOME
Den Kopf des Jochanaan.

HERODES
Das sagst du nur, um mich zu quälen,
weil ich dich so angeschaut habe.
Deine Schönheit hat mich verwirrt.
Oh! Oh! Bringt Wein! Mich dürstet!
Salome, Salome, lass uns wie Freunde
zu einander sein! Bedenk' dich! Ah!
Was wollt ich sagen? Was war's? Ah!
Ich weiss es wieder! Salome, du
kennst meine weissen Pfauen, meine
schönen weissen Pfauen, die im Garten zwischen den Myrten wandeln.
Ich will sie dir alle, alle geben. In
der ganzen Welt lebt kein König, der
solche Pfauen hat. Ich habe bloss
hundert. Aber alle will ich dir geben.

(*Er leert seinen Becher*)

SALOME
Gib mir den Kopf des Jochanaan!

HERODIAS
Gut gesagt, meine Tochter!
(*zu Herodes*)
Und du, du bist lächerlich mit deinen
Pfauen.

HERODES
Still, Weib! Du kreischest wie ein
Raubvogel. Deine Stimme peinigt
mich. Still sag' ich dir! Salome, bedenk, was du tun willst. Es kann sein,
dass der Mann von Gott gesandt ist.
Er ist ein heil'ger Mann. Der Finger

SALOME (*rising, laughing*)

The head of Jokanaan.

HEROD (*rising abruptly*)

No! No!

HERODIAS

Ah! That you said well, my daughter! That you said well.

HEROD

No, no, Salome; do you not ask that of me. Do not heed the counsel of your mother. Your mother has an evil tongue. Pay no heed to her.

SALOME

I pay no heed to the voice of my mother. It is to please myself that I want the head of Jokanaan, and in a silver vessel, Tetrarch. Remember the oath you've taken, Herod. Remember the oath you've taken. Do not forget!

HEROD (*hastily*)

I know, I know it was an oath I've taken, I know it well. By all that's holy I have made this promise. But I do beseech you, Salome, I beg of you, ask anything else. I'll gladly bestow upon you half my realm, I'll gladly bestow it. But, do not ask me, do not ask me what your lips have just spoken!

SALOME (*strongly*)

Give me the head of Jokanaan!

HEROD

No, no, that I will never give you!

SALOME

Remember the oath you've taken, Herod.

HERODIAS

Yes, remember the oath you've taken. All bear witness to the fact.

HEROD

Silence, woman. My words were not to you.

HERODIAS

But my daughter did well to ask for that: The head of Jokanaan. Let her have it. He's sullied my name with slander and filth. How she loves her mother is plain to see. Make him pay, my dear daughter, make him pay. Remember the oath he's taken.

HEROD

Silence! Speak not to me. Salome, I implore you: Be not wilful, child. And have I not always loved you well? Perhaps I may have loved too well, my dear. Therefore be prudent; ask not for this. You never must witness how a head is severed from a living body. Heed what I say! I have a flawless em'rald. It is the fairest em'rald in all the world. Can you resist such a prize? But ask it of me, and it shall be given, this fairest em'rald.

SALOME

I ask for the head of Jokanaan!

HEROD

You pay no heed, you pay no heed! Be silent and listen, Salome.

SALOME

The head of Jokanaan!

HEROD

I understand. You want to trick me because I gazed at you often. Your beauty dazzled my eyes. O! O! Bring wine, I'm thirsty! Salome, Salome, let us not quarrel with each other so. But listen! Ah! What would I tell you? But wait! Ah, now I remember! Salome, you know of my famous peacocks, of my peacocks, white and wond'rous? In my garden you must have seen them wand'ring. To you I'll give every single peacock! Throughout all the world not a king who can boast of peacocks like mine. I have a full hundred. To you all of them shall be given.

(*He empties the cup of wine.*)

SALOME

Give me the head of Jokanaan!

HERODIAS

That is good, my daughter!

(*to Herod*)

But you, you're ridiculous with all your peacocks!

HEROD

Silence! You're screeching like a bird of prey. How your voice tortures me! Silence, I say . . . Salome, but think what you're doing. People say of this man that God has sent him . . . He is a holy man. He is a prophet whom

Gottes hat ihn berührt. Du möchtest nicht, dass mich ein Unheil trifft, Salome? Hör' jetzt auf mich!

SALOME

Ich will den Kopf des Jochanaan!

HERODES (auffahrend)

Ach! Du willst nicht auf mich hören. Sei ruhig, Salome. Ich, siehst du, bin ruhig. Höre:

(leise und heimlich)

Ich habe an diesem Ort Juwelen versteckt, Juwelen, die selbst deine Mutter nie gesehen hat. Ich habe ein Halsband mit vier Reihen Perlen, Topase, gelb wie die Augen der Tiger. Topase, hellrot wie die Augen der Waldtaube, und grüne Topase, wie Katzenaugen. Ich habe Opale, die immer funkeln, mit einem Feuer, kalt wie Eis. Ich will sie dir alle geben, alle!

(immer aufgeregter)

Ich habe Chrysolithe und Berylle, Chrysoprase und Rubine. Ich habe Sardonyx-und Hyazinthsteine und Steine von Chalcedon. Ich will sie dir alle geben, alle und noch andere Dinge. Ich habe einen Kristall, in den zu schaun keinem Weibe vergönnt ist. Iin einem Perlmutterkästchen habe ich drei wunderbare Türkise: Wer sie an seiner Stirne trägt, kann Dinge sehn, die nicht wirklich sind. Es sind unbezahlbare Schätze. Was begehrst du sonst noch, Salome? Alles, was du verlangst, will ich dir geben — nur eines nicht: Nur nicht das Leben dieses einen Mannes. Ich will dir den Mantel des Hohenpriesters geben. Ich will dir den Vorhang des Allerheiligsten geben.

DIE JUDEN

Oh, oh, oh!

SALOME (wild)

Gib mir den Kopf des Jochanaan!

(Herodes sinkt verzweifelt auf seinen Sitz zurück.)

HERODES (matt)

Man soll ihr geben, was sie verlangt! Sie ist in Wahrheit ihrer Mutter Kind!

(Herodias zieht dem Tetrarchen den Todesring vom Finger und gibt ihn dem ersten Soldaten, der ihn auf der Stelle dem Henker überbringt.)

Wer hat meinen Ring genommen?

(Der Henker geht in die Cisterne hinab.)

Ich hatte einen Ring an meiner rechten Hand. Wer hat meinen Wein getrunken? Es war Wein in meinem Becher. Er war mit Wein gefüllt. Es hat ihn jemand ausgetrunken.

(leise)

Gewiss wird Unheil über einen kommen.

HERODIAS

Meine Tochter hat recht getan!

HERODES

Ich bin sicher, es wird ein Unheil geschehn.

SALOME

(an der Cisterne lauschend)

Es ist kein Laut zu vernehmen. Ich höre nichts. Warum schreit er nicht, der Mann? Ah! Wenn einer mich zu töten käme, ich würde schreien, ich würde mich wehren, ich würde es nicht dulden! Schlag zu, schlag zu, Naaman, schlag zu, sag ich dir! Nein, ich höre nichts.

(gedehnt)

Es ist eine schreckliche Stille! Ah! Es ist etwas zu Boden gefallen. Ich hörte etwas fallen. Es war das Schwert des Henkers. Er hat Angst, dieser Sklave. Er hat das Schwert fallen lassen! Er traut sich nicht, ihn zu töten. Er ist eine Memme, dieser Sklave. Schickt Soldaten hin!

(zum Pagen)

Komm hierher, du warst der Freund dieses Toten, nicht? Wohlan, ich sage dir: Es sind noch nicht genug Tote. Geh zu den Soldaten und befiehl ihnen, hinabzusteigen und mir zu holen, was ich verlange, was der Tetrarch mir versprochen hat, was mein ist!

(Der Page weicht zurück, sie wendet sich den Soldaten zu.)

Hierher, ihr Soldaten, geht ihr in die Cisterne hinunter und holt mir den Kopf des Mannes!

God hath touched. How could you wish that harm should come to me, Salome? Heed what I say!

SALOME

Give me the head of Jokanaan!

HEROD (*irritated*)

Ah . . . you will not, you will not listen. Be calm, Salome! I, you see, am calm. Now, listen.

(*softly and secretively*)

I have a secret place where jewels are hid, yes, jewels that even your mother has never seen. I've hidden a necklace with four strands of pearls. I've sapphires blue as the waves of the ocean. A topaz, yellow as the eyes of the wild tiger. And gorgeous emeralds green, green as cats' eyes. And I have an opal that burns and sparkles with a flame as cold as ice . . . To you shall all these jewels be given; I swear it.

(*with still more agitation*)

I have the rarest chrysolites and fine beryls. Chrysoprases and spark'ling rubies. I have fine sardonyx and brilliant hyacinths and bracelets of chalcedony. To you shall they all be given, all that you could wish for. A mystic crystal ball that is forbidden for woman to gaze on, a pair of turquoise amulets are hidden in a casket covered with garnets, and he who wears them on his forehead can behold things which never were. These are priceless treasures I offer. Can you long for ought else, Salome? All of them shall be your own. I'll gladly give you all, save one thing . . . But do not ask me for the head of this man . . . I'll give you the mantle, the mantle of the high priest, I'll give you the veil hanging on the Holy of Holies . . .

THE JEWS

Oh! Oh! Oh!

SALOME (*wildly*)

Give me the head of Jokanaan!

(*Herod, in despair, sinks back in his seat.*)

HEROD (*faintly*)

Let her be given what she demands! She is for certain her mother's child.

(*Herodias draws from the hand of the Tetrarch the ring of death and gives it to the soldier, who immediately bears it to the executioner.*)

Who took the ring from my hand?

(*The executioner goes down into the cistern.*)

I am sure I had the ring. I had it on my hand . . . and now my goblet's empty . . . There was wine in my goblet. There was wine in it. Someone has taken it all . . .

(*faintly*)

Oh! I know misfortune will come down upon us!

HERODIAS

My daughter's done well indeed!

HEROD

I am certain that some misfortune will come.

SALOME

(*listening at the cistern*)

There's not a sound from the cistern. No, not a sound . . . Why does he not cry out, this man? . . . Ah! If it were I they came to kill, how I would struggle! My cries would be fearful. I know I would not suffer! Now strike, now strike, Naaman, and now strike, I say! No, I hear nothing.

(*hesitatingly*)

There is a terrible silence. Ah! Something has fallen to the ground. I heard something falling. It is the sword of the headsman . . . He is frightened, this coward! He's dropped his sword in his terror! He will not strike, he is frightened. He is such a coward, slave and weakling. Send the soldiers down!

(*to the page*)

Come hither. You were the friend of this dead man, yes? Well then, I say to you we do not have enough dead men. Order all the soldiers to descend into the cistern at once that they may bring me that which I long for, that which the Tetrarch has sworn an oath to give me!

(*The page recoils. Salome turns to the soldiers.*)

Come hither, you soldiers. Go down into this cistern and hurry! Now, bring me the head of the prophet!

(schreiend)

Tetrarch, Tetrarch, befiehl deinen Soldaten, dass sie mir den Kopf des
Jochanaan holen!

*(Ein riesengrosser schwarzer Arm, der
Arm des Henkers, streckt sich aus der
Cisterne heraus, auf einem silbernen
Schild den Kopf des Jochanaan
haltend. Salome ergreift ihn. Herodes
verhüllt sein Gesicht mit dem Mantel. Herodias fächelt sich zu und
lächelt. Die Nazarener sinken in die
Knie und beginnen zu beten.)*

Ah! Du wolltest mich nicht deinen
Mund küssen lassen, Jochanaan!
Wohl, ich werde ihn jetzt küssen!
Ich will mit meinen Zähnen hinein-
beissen, wie man in eine reife Frucht
beissen mag. Ja, ich will ihn jetzt
küssen, deinen Mund, Jochanaan.
Ich hab' es gesagt. Hab' ich's nicht
gesagt? Ja, ich hab' es gesagt. Ah!
Ah! Ich will ihn jetzt küssen. Aber
warum siehst du mich nicht an, Jochanaan? Deine Augen, die so schrecklich waren, so voller Wut und
Verachtung, sind jetzt geschlossen.
Warum sind sie geschlossen? Oeffne
doch die Augen, erhebe deine Lider,
Jochanaan! Warum siehst du mich
nicht an? Hast du Angst vor mir,
Jochanaan, dass du mich nicht an-
sehen willst? Und deine Zunge, sie
spricht kein Wort, Jochanaan, diese
Scharlachnatter, die ihren Geifer gegen mich spie. Es ist seltsam, nicht?
Wie kommt es, dass diese rote Natter
sich nicht mehr rührt? Du sprachst
böse Worte gegen mich, gegen mich,
Salome, die Tochter der Herodias,
Prinzessin von Judäa. Nun wohl! Ich
lebe noch, aber du bist tot, und dein
Kopf, dein Kopf gehört mir! Ich
kann mit ihm tun, was ich will. Ich
kann ihn den Hunden vorwerfen und
den Vögeln der Luft. Was die Hunde
übrig lassen, sollen die Vögel der
Luft verzehren. Ah! Ah! Jochanaan,
Jochanaan, du warst schön. Dein
Leib war eine Elfenbeinsäule auf
silbernen Füssen. Er war ein Garten
voller Tauben in der Silberlilien
Glanz. Nichts in der Welt war so
weiss wie dein Leib. Nichts in der
Welt war so schwarz wie dein Haar.
In der ganzen Welt war nichts so rot
wie dein Mund. Deine Stimme war
ein Weihrauchgefäss, und wenn ich

dich ansah, hörte ich geheimnisvolle
Musik.

*(in den Anblick von Jochanaans Haupt
versunken)*

Ah! Warum hast du mich nicht angesehn, Jochanaan? Du legtest über
deine Augen die Binde eines, der seinen Gott schauen wollte. Wohl! Du
hast deinen Gott gesehn, Jochanaan,
aber mich, mich hast du nie gesehn.
Hättest du mich gesehn, du hättest
mich geliebt! Ich dürste nach deiner
Schönheit. Ich hungre nach deinem
Leib. Nicht Wein noch Aepfel können mein Verlangen stillen. Was soll
ich jetzt tun, Jocnanaan? Nicht die
Fluten, noch die grossen Wasser können dieses brünstige Begehren löschen. Oh! Warum sahst du mich
nicht an? Hättest du mich angesehn,
du hättest mich geliebt. Ich weiss es
wohl, du hättest mich geliebt. Und
das Geheimnis der Liebe ist grösser
als das Geheimnis des Todes.

HERODES *(leise zu Herodias)*

Sie ist ein Ungeheuer, deine Tochter.
Ich sage dir, sie ist ein Ungeheuer!

HERODIAS *(stark)*

Sie hat recht getan. Ich möchte jetzt
hier bleiben.

HERODES *(steht auf)*

Ah! Da spricht meines Bruders Weib!

(schwächer)

Komm, ich will nicht an diesem Orte
bleiben.

(heftig)

Komm, sag' ich dir! Sicher, es wird
Schreckliches geschehn. Wir wollen
uns im Palast verbergen, Herodias,
ich fange an zu erzittern.

(Der Mond verschwindet.)
(auffahrend)

Manassah, Issachar, Ozias, lösch die
Fackeln aus. Verbergt den Mond,
verbergt die Sterne! Es wird Schreckliches geschehn.

*(Die Sklaven löschen die Fackeln aus.
Die Sterne verschwinden. Eine grosse
Wolke zieht über den Mond und
verhüllt ihn völlig. Die Bühne wird
ganz dunkel. Der Tetrarch beginnt
die Treppe hinaufzusteigen.)*

(shouting)

Tetrarch! Tetrarch! Command some of your soldiers that they bring me the head of Jokanaan.

(A huge black arm, the arm of the executioner, comes forth from the cistern, bearing on a silver shield the head of Jokanaan. Salome seizes it. Herod hides his face with his cloak. Herodias smiles and fans herself. The Nazarenes fall on their knees and begin to pray.)

Ah! Why did you not let me but kiss, kiss your sweet mouth, Jokanaan! Ah, ah yes, now I will kiss it. And with my teeth I'll bite it. I will bite it as one would bite a fruit that's ripe, ripe and fresh. Yes, see I will now kiss it, kiss your mouth, Jokanaan . . . I said that I would . . . You heard, did you not? Yes, I say it again. Ah! Ah! See I will now kiss it. Ah, but why do you close your eyes, Jokanaan? Your eyes that were so terrifying, so full of rage and of fire, why are they shut now? Oh, wherefore have you shut them? Let your eyes be open, your eyes which did despise me, Jokanaan! Oh why do you close your eyes? Are you afraid of me, Jokanaan? Why do you not want to look on me? Your tongue is quiet, it speaks no more, Jokanaan, such a scarlet viper which spat its venom upon me. It is strange though, ah, how is it that this small scarlet vipor does stir no more? You spoke evil words against me then, against me, Salome, the daughter of Herodias, the Princess of Judaea! Well then! I'm living still; ah, but you are dead! And your head . . . your head belongs to me! I'm free to do with it what I will. I'll give it to dogs to feed upon, and the birds in the air. If the dogs should leave a little, then let the birds of the air devour it . . . Ah! Ah! Jokanaan! Jokanaan! You were fair! . . . Your body was a tower of silver decked with shields of ivory. It was a garden full of wood doves where the silver lilies glow. Nothing on earth was so white as your skin. Nothing on earth was so black as your hair. There is naught in all the world so red as your mouth. And your voice was like perfume of flowers. And when I looked on you

I could hear a strange and glorious song.

(lost in thought as she gazes upon Jokanaan's head)

Ah! But why did you never look at me, Jokanaan? You laid over both your eyes the perfect blindfold of one who seeks the vision of God. Well, your God you have seen at last, Jokanaan. But me, me, me you shall .never see. If you had looked on me, you would have found me fair. I thirst for your manly beauty; I hunger to touch your flesh. Not wine nor apples can appease my fierce desire. What shall I do now, Jokanaan? Neither waters nor the raging torrents could ever quench my burning, searing passion. Oh! But why did you look away? Had you but looked on my face you would have loved me too! Yes, I am sure you would have loved me too. And the great mystery of loving is greater than the mystery of dying

HEROD *(softly to Herodias)*

She is a fearful monster, your daughter. I say to you she is a monster.

HERODIAS *(strongly)*

No. My daughter was right, I say. And I want to stay here now.

HEROD *(rising)*

Ah! There speaks my brother's wife.

(weaker)

Come, I will not remain a moment longer.

(vehemently)

Come, come I say! Surely, something terrible will happen. Let us hide ourselves within the palace. Herodias, I'm beginning to tremble . . .

(The moon disappears.)

(vehemently)

Manasseh, Isacher, Ozias, put the torches out! Go, hide the stars! And hide the moonlight! Something terrible will come!

(The slaves put out the torches. The stars disappear. A great cloud crosses the moon and conceals it completely. The scene becomes quite dark. The Tetrarch begins to climb the staircase.)

SALOME (*matt*)

Ah! Ich habe deinen Mund geküsst,
Jochanaan. Ah! Ich habe ihn geküsst
deinen Mund, es war ein bitterer
Geschmack auf deinen Lippen. Hat
es nach Blut geschmeckt? Nein!
Doch es schmeckte vielleicht nach
Liebe. Sie sagen, dass die Liebe bitter
schmecke. Allein, was tut's? Was tut's?
Ich habe deinen Mund geküsst, Joch-
anaan. Ich habe ihn geküsst, deinen
Mund.

(*Der Mond bricht wieder hervor und
beleuchtet Salome.*)

HERODES (*sich umwendend*)

Man töte dieses Weib!

(*Die Soldaten stürzen sich auf Salome
und begraben sie unter ihren
Schilden.*)

ENDE

SALOME (*faintly*)

Ah! I now at last have kissed your mouth, Jokanaan. Ah! I now at last have kissed your mouth. There was a bitter taste upon your lips. Was it the taste of blood? Nay! But perchance is it thus that love tastes? They say that the taste of love is bitter . . . I pay no heed . . . no heed . . . I have now kissed your mouth, Jokanaan. I have impressed a kiss upon your mouth.

(*A ray of moonlight falls on Salome and illumines her.*)

HEROD (*turning around*)

That woman must be killed!

(*The soldiers rush forward and crush Salome beneath their shields.*)

THE END